T0266264

Lockdown Parenting FAILS*

Lockdown Parenting FAILS*

*(because it's not all f**king rainbows)

Compiled by
Nathan Joyce

Published by Welbeck
An imprint of Welbeck Non-Fiction Limited,
part of Welbeck Publishing Group.
20 Mortimer Street,
London W1T 3JW

First published by Welbeck in 2020

A CIP catalogue record for this book is available from the British Library

ISBN
Hardback – 9781787395787
eBook – 9781787395794

Typeset by EnvyDesign
Cover design by Alexandra Allden
Cover and internal illustration by Emma Scully
Printed in the UK

10 9 8 7 6 5 4 3 2 1

www.welbeckpublishing.com

For the parents – gold stars all round.

Contents

Introduction ix

Chapter 1:
Homeschooling Horror Show 1

Chapter 2:
WFH WTF 35

Chapter 3:
Kitchen Nightmares 65

Chapter 4:
Healthy Body, Healthy Mind 93

Chapter 5:
Musings 119

Acknowledgements 145

About the Author 148

Introduction

Back in March, I was a new parent with a five-month-old. I'm not sure who was flailing around more frantically, me or little Finn, him trying to explore everything and me trying to stop him from swallowing pen lids, bottle caps and Maltesers that we have strewn about in our non-baby-proofed bio-hazard of a house. And then just as we'd secured the lounge, lockdown happened and we were basically confined to that room for the next few weeks. The outside world was limited to David Attenborough documentaries, and our only human contact involved waving at the postman through the window.

One frustratingly samey lockdown afternoon in early April, I discovered Twitter, a mere 14 years late. It felt daring, like I'd just taken the red pill in *The Matrix* (wait – that's the fun one, right?). I happened across a Tweet from the spectacular @muminbits and I thought "hang on – that sounds a bit like what I want to say, only much funnier".

Reading fellow parents' stories and anecdotes as they navigated the lockdown hurdles of homeschooling, working from home and trying to keep the kids entertained was hilarious but also really cathartic. I wasn't the only one swigging gin from the bottle, hoovering up biscuits and trying to avoid looking up either my screen time notification or step count. We were all cocking things up! And there were parents coping with not just one, but multiple mini wrecking balls and not only surviving, but laughing about it. These folks are my heroes.

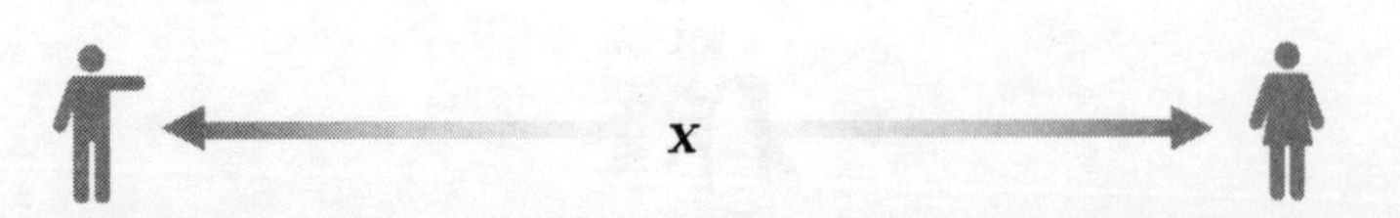

So I thought of compiling a book of lockdown parenting fails that we could look back and laugh at. At the very least, it can be used for emergency toilet paper.

CHAPTER 1

Homeschooling HorrorShow

PRE-LOCKDOWN MENTALITY: teaching's easy, right? A week off in February and October, two weeks off at Christmas and Easter and six weeks off in the summer. What a bunch of loungers.
During lockdown: *would eat words but have forgotten how to write*

In our new roles as professional teachers, we're winging it. We're all in the same (sinking) (life)boat (with no life jacket). Our bar for what can be achieved in a day has fallen spectacularly. Kids still alive at end of day? Pass the ice cream!

So what if the kids have learned nothing during lockdown? We've learned loads! We've learned that teachers don't get paid enough, discovered that a 30-minute lesson can feel

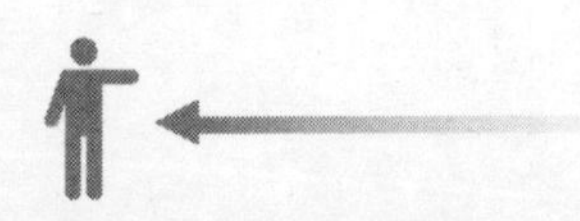

like a day and a half and agree that Disney+ is perfectly educational. But perhaps most importantly, we've realised that no hour is too early to start drinking during lockdown.

In this chapter, you'll find that most parents (myself very much included) have lost the plot during lockdown – some quite gloriously. We're all drinking heavily and hoping the kids don't find us when we hide in the toilet for a moment's peace (and for enough time to hoover up a Wispa).

Some high-flying few are genuinely winning (well, sort of), but we all get gold stars for effort.

LOST THE PLOT

Christ, it's been a long week. Let's open that wine*

* Monday, 3pm

@Debs_surfs, 30 March

One major plus of homeschooling so far: I'm finally weaning myself off coffee...
...and onto gin.

@helen_tovey11, 3 April

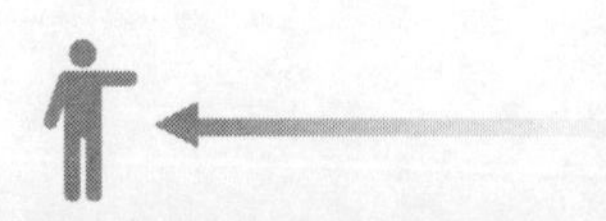

An espresso martini counts as a morning coffee break, right?

@andreaktv, 15 April

Always wondered what teachers carried in their rucksacks. Based on my first two weeks of homeschooling experience, I'd say tequila and a taser.

@amanda_pilsen23, 16 April

I've taught 11 year olds, 15 year olds and A-level students for years. So how am I coping with homeschooling two kids under 7?

I'm drinking gin from the bottle. LIKE EVERYONE ELSE.

@nicolaegham99, 15 May

Day 2 homeschooling.
#everyhouseholdrightnow

@hove_aboard, 24 March

Sentences I never thought I'd say to my five year old son before lockdown:
"No, it's not ok to paint a rainbow on your willy to support the NHS."

@number50CT, 10 June

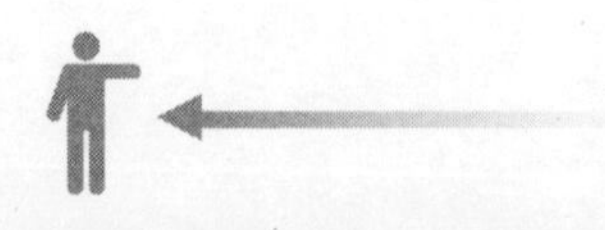

Is it acceptable to tip your kids' teachers at parent's evenings from now on?

@shop0holic, 30 May

Daddy, why can't we find a bigger virus to eat coronavirus?
I'm not sure if I've spent too long in quarantine or I've spent too long listening to shambolic government daily briefings, but that really makes sense to me.

@dadtotwodaughters, 10 May

If it takes a village to raise a child that village better have a f**king gin factory.

@phoebs_silverback, 11 May

After 3 hours sleep and a full day of saying "put it back, stop hitting George and don't feed the dog ice cream" my parenting skills have somewhat diminished. So when the following exchange happened, I wasn't prepared.

7 year old: "George just pooed a lego man"
Me: Put it back!
Me:(five seconds later) No, WAIT!

@chasgrumman1, 22 June

Mummy, is it called gronavirus cos only grownups get it?
Me: Possibly

@k00kykaty, 16 June

Think I lost it today.

4 yo: "How do you make maple syrup?"
Me: "You have to squeeze loads of Canadian flags together."

@fathertoted, 3 June

Got my first parents evening tonight. F**k knows what I'm gonna tell this idiot's folks. He's a lost cause.

@bmw_m5man, 1 June

Walking downstairs during a break from work, I overheard my wife say:
"Alexa, homeschool the children."
Fair.

@dan_jardine86, 20 April

Yeah, no problem, I'll help with long division, just as soon as I'm back from the toilet.

frantically looks up tutorial on YouTube from toilet
#everyparent

@bossmansboss, 2 April

Day 3 of homeschooling and we're already on a supply teacher.
"Kids, Mr Disney has kindly decided to step in at short notice."

@andy_dangerscott, 10 April

I regret telling my 6 year old to go paint something for art class. I think the cat does as well.

@annie_myers1986, 14 May

How To
Survive
Home work
(For Parents)
Times
Tables
6 + 7 =
12 ÷ 2 =
9 × 6 =
16 - 14
123 × 2

Day 1 of homeschooling, lesson one. Hand goes up.
"I'd like to see the lunch menu mummy."

@aliloupet, 29 March

5 year old: Daddy you're the best teacher ever!
7 year old: Daddy you're the WORST teacher ever!

That's a 50% success rate. I'll take it.

@BertTRaines, 5 May

School's out but the life lessons continue... Today we learned what happens when you leave two bananas in the basement for a month.

@JeninLdnont, 26 June

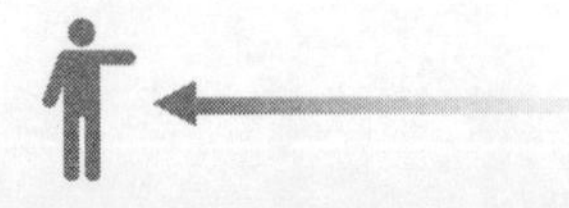

Banning screen time is like the nuclear deterrent. Carrying out the threat leads to mutually assured destruction.

@tim_fordyce, 11 April

Today, I've spent the first three hours of homeschooling observing and treating Lego people for symptoms of coronavirus.

@andrea_topp, 15 May

My homeschooling kitchen has got more broken pencils in it than a urologist's waiting room.

@dad_o_rail, 11 May

Can't wait for the OFSTED inspection. This school is gonna close!

@samrickard, 17 June

MARKS FOR EFFORT

6 year old switched the hoover on and stuck it through the letterbox screaming: "Got you stinky virus!"

Certainly gave the postman a fright.

@mahmood_adil, 22 May

Daddy I think the virus started in Germany. That's where the germs live. (Could have corrected him, but he sounded confident. And who the f*** knows anything anymore.)

@braindad, 3 April

I managed to shepherd a bee out of the classroom during homeschooling today. Looked round, pleased with myself.

Rapidly inconsolable 5 year old: "That was my best best friend in the whole world. I HATE YOU NEW TEACHER."

@nicki north11, 8 May

5yo managed to call and get through to an HSBC operator today...

...to try and cash in her "Bank error in your favour" Monopoly card.

@raj_katy44, 3 May

Dad's been "handling" homeschooling art class this morning.

@bfg20002001, 28 March

Homeschooling lesson today was about what you want to do when you're older.
The answers are in:

6 year old: Astronaut
5 year old: A "sweet eater"
3 year old: A dinosaur!

This teaching shizzle is a doddle.

@litlou23, 24 April

Spent an hour today explaining to my five year old why lego Darth Vader was uniquely placed to not catch coronavirus.

5 year old: "Is he a hero then daddy?"

I wasn't expecting parenting questions to be this hard.

@mayhem77, 1 July

Day 23 of homeschooling and losing the plot:

Me: "Kids, only one thing for you to do for today's music class (*holds up Nirvana CD*): I want you to write the lyrics to the song *Smells Like Teen Spirit* (thought to self: ha ha – that'll keep them occupied for hours! I'm not sure Kurt Cobain knew what the hell he was saying).

email arrives 5 mins later
https://genius.com/Nirvana-smells-like-teen-spirit-lyrics

@needlenose_ned, 5 May

Me: Are you... praying?
10 year old: I'm asking God for another teacher next year.

@life_overrated, 28 June

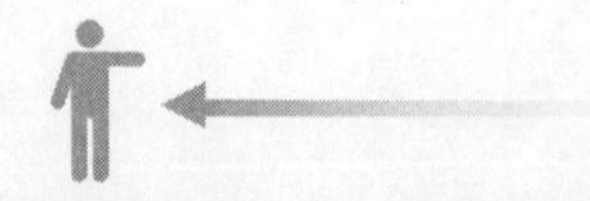

How was homeschooling today Lydia?

Oscar's Homeschool Report Card

Oscar is an idiot!!

Signed,
MUM

Me: What are you doing?
7 year old: Jumping on the bed – it's our PE class!

@1978katmcgraw, 11 May

Genuine question: "Can you freeze a fart in the freezer daddy?"
Thought he was a moron, but I don't know – can you?

@rob_dallas1, 14 April

HAND ME THE THERAPY BILL

6 year old: Why don't islands sink?
Me: Because they're inflatable.

@ClaireTallis2, 29 March

8yo daughter: If kids have milk teeth what do adults have?
Wine teeth.

@beckyschofield44, 26 May

Daddy, daddy, daddy! (5 year old says running in, breathless)

Yes...

How do mermaids poo?

They don't, but they fart so hard it shoots them out of the water

(*did I really just say that?*)

@originaldadbod, 4 May

Daughter asked me what WIFI stood for today.

"The end of meaningful interaction". I told her.

@frisby_sam, 13 April

"How are teachers not all alcoholics?!"

@sammyJwright, March 29

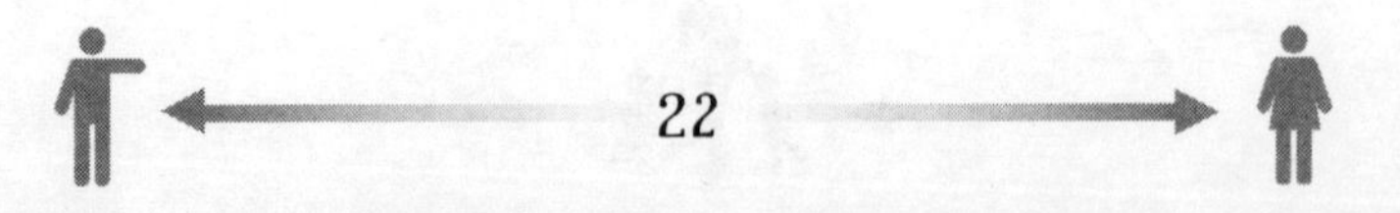

Day 11 of homeschooling: learning about the role of the American president.
Kid: What does Washington DC stand for?
Me: Douchebag City.

@r_a_p_scallion, 22 May

[Overheard conversation between 5 year old son and 4 year old daughter]
4 year old: If I was in mummy's tummy, that means you were in daddy's tummy.
5 year old: Who's in there now then?
Me (too loudly): Budweiser.

@momwillshoot, 29 June

[Overheard conversation between hubby and 6 year old daughter (we live in Texas)]
6 year old: Dad, where's Ohio?
Husband: Up and right a bit.

@michaeltodonohue 14 June

HURRY up!! EXAMS Nearly Over!!
It needs to go to the tax man.. ...er I mean ... ..TEACHER!!!!
JULY
31
HOME SCHOOL
KS4 MATH
TAX RETURN
HELP!!!

What's the difference between a solid, a liquid and a gas?
Me: PLOP, PEE, PARP
7 year old: Euuuurghghhhhh!

@tazwickham, 30 March

If me and Maisy both came from mummy's tummy, did Finn come from Finland?
Me: Yes. Yes he did.

@claretaverner, 25 May

4 year old: Daddy, can we go to the playground yet?
Hubby (tired): Oh sorry Lou, the virus has, er, eaten it.

@5678SusieStepp, 15 April

WINNING

Found some graffiti on my kitchen table this morning. It reads:
Mr Armstrong is a nob.
Rather than reprimand anyone, I've amended it to:
Mr Armstrong is a noble soul teaching a couple of oiks.

@Armstrong_jakey1982, 6 May

Me: do you think I'm a good teacher?
3yo: no.
Me: well you're 3 no one cares what you think.

@daddydoubts, 14 May

New class timetable Monday morning (pinned on the fridge) –
Period 1 Geography: discovering where the laundry basket and washing machine are.
Period 2 Music: listening to the melodious hum of kids hoovering.
Period 3 Animal Science: walking the dog.

@euanryoungs, 22 April

Watching *Outbreak* definitely counts as Science class, right?

@thedudeabld3s, 30 March

4 yo: How do you make chocolate?
Me: The Easter Bunny poos it out. Then the farmer collects it in a bucket, like he does with milk.
4 yo *Puts down mini mars bar*
Me: YOINK!

@dad_ringer, 20 April

5 year old: Why's it called sand?
Me: Er, because you find it between the sea and the land.
(I think that might be the most insightful thing I've ever said.)

@sandy_schmitt10, 11 May

I'm Sure We Can Find You Something to Read Timmy, Er.....
?
?

50 SHADES OF GREY
Gone girl
Why mummy drinks
The Shining
50 SHADES DARKER
The Book of C*nts

My wife, who has quite a talent for accents, just prank called our landline pretending to be an OFSTED inspector checking "homeschooling standards".

I completely bought it and apologised for everything. Only realised it was her when she told me she'd "be fining my ass".

@Stu_beefA4K009, 6 May

So impressed with my kid's new teacher that I've bought her a present.

ADDS ALL THE THINGS IN WISH LIST TO BASKET.

@allbetsyareoff, 29 March

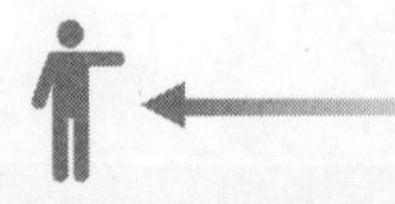

If I set off the smoke alarm, can I get away with insisting my kids don't come back in the house until I give them the all clear? In like 5 hours?

@lifeofphil, 23 March

Nana usually looks after the kids for one day a week and helps with homework. Lockdown's been with us for 14 weeks.

The way I see it, Nana owes me 14 days. Hubby and I off on holiday!

@Alex_lumos00, 2 April

10 year old: Mummy, didn't you say once that homeschooled children are really weird?
Me: Er yes, and I stand by my former statement.

@sandy_schmitt10, 21 May

So there's been a lot of Disney during lockdown for our 7 and 5 year olds and I've realised the educational lessons they're learning:

Aladdin – Thievery and lying pays.
Tangled – Run away with a known fugitive who breaks into your house.
Lion King – Run away from home and piss about in a commune.
Snow White – Cook and clean for seven old men

I'm fine with that.

@don_darko888, 24 May

Wait, we got to write their report cards this term, right, given that we're their teachers now?
Also, it's ok to just write "prick" isn't it?
Asking for a friend.

@jasmeet_RI, 12 May

Coloring with Mom vs. coloring with Dad

pickled.plutonium, 9 April

CHAPTER 2

WFH WTF

A FEW MONTHS AGO, "working from home" was code for "I'm drinking beer and playing frisbee in the park" and Zoom was a phallic ice lolly from the '80s. Everything's changed. Now many of us are saying "God I miss the commute". That's a sentence that you never thought you'd utter, up there with "I miss the toilets at Glastonbury" or "I fancy another root canal".

During lockdown, working from home presents us with new hurdles to scramble over. Now we all flail around frantically at the end of the Zoom meeting trying to avoid being the last to press the "Leave" button. And that's just without kids. Add a five-year-old who can't find their unicorn and is confronted by a locked door, and we're at DEFCON 1.

How we all rolled about back in 2017 when US academic Robert Kelly was interviewed by the BBC. The door to his study opens dramatically and Kelly's four-year-old daughter bounds up to her daddy's desk, pursued by a toddler on a rolling chair. After a few seconds, the children's mother, Jung-a-Kim, who had been trying to film the interview on their TV in the living room, is seen flailing around desperately on her hands and knees to retrieve the children, scooping them into the corridor and closing the door. The whole scene resembles a live pantomime. "Usually I lock the door. This time I forgot," said a downcast Kelly afterwards, assuming his career was over. We feel your pain, Robert!

A week later, the video had been watched 36 million times and the Kellys were dubbed "the most famous family in America". Robert's Twitter profile now includes: "that BBC Dad guy (yes, really)".

So, embrace the carnage. You don't know where it might lead. We're in this together.

COPING WITH NEW COLLEAGUES

WFH day 1: managed to whisper "YOU LOOK HOT" loudly into what turned out to be my husband's live meeting headset mic.

@wfhmaestro, 23 March

Today I found myself yelling "Get that Play Dough out of your brother's ear" and "A cat is not a dart board" on a Zoom call. #wfhwinning

@AngelaD5900, 8 June

I've just had to mute myself on a conference call to yell "DON'T SLIDE DOWN THE STAIRS IN THE BASKET" through the spare room door. I miss my office.

@whatKatydidnext, 1 July

Starting to think wfh is affecting my kids. My 3 year old daughter now holds the receiver of her fake phone in one hand and yells "I'm on a call now, Mummy"

@Rabbit_headlights1990, 28 June

So my daughter decided today to dry her collage using not one but two hairdryers using the plug socket outside my office.

@Nat_express, 28 May

I was delivering an online lecture on astrophysics today and out of the corner of my eye I saw my 5 year old walk in carrying my vuvuzela. I've never experienced fear like it.

@Starkerscharkers, 29 April

A colleague just overheard me saying "please leave your undies on darling, you will get sand in your crack" (to my toddler).

@andy_park, 17 April

Me 5 minutes ago: omg... I've been hacked! seriously hackers, can't you give us a break? {scrambles to change entire digital life, hoping my identity isn't stolen} Me now: Turns out my 2 year old son was messing with my bluetooth mouse in another room.

@ryevenbark, 26 March

Just finished presenting a Zoom meeting with my four-year-old yelling "Daddy's boring" through the keyhole.

@hesalldad, 15 April

04:14 pm
ZOOM
LIVE
VIDEO CALL
BY: EMMA

Audible to colleagues of a Google Hangout: "My willy fell off and my daddy doesn't care". Wondering if I'll get arrested.

@ ttf_2253747, 10 April

Walked into my study today to find that my 5 year old daughter had stuck post-it notes on every single visible object each of which had a brief description.

My favourite was the middle of the chair, labelled "Where Daddy farts".

@55andy_hayward, 3 April

So in my desk drawer, there's a cheeky stash of biscuits hidden in a lever arch file. Found a little note on it this morning covered in crumbs which read: "I'm onto you, Daddy".

@neilsmith1977, 18 May

Found this threatening note slipped under my door during a Zoom meeting. This is what life has come to.

Culprit: child at kitchen table with blue pen marks on hands and face.

@haisha99, 30 Jun

Received an email this morning from my boss which read: "Sorry to hear about that, Jim! Take as much time as you need."

Took me some time to work out as I hadn't messaged him for about a week. Finally looked in my sent items and found a message my daughter had written him:
"Daddy can't work – he has a smelly bum."

@winging_parenting, 16 May

I'm a teacher and do a lot of marking at home so my desk is covered in little red splodges. Found them all this morning covered in plasters with "ouchy" on them.

@savedby_the_bell, 26 March

Zoom call contribution from reprobate 6 year old: "Mummy, why does Daddy have boobies too?" Colleagues prefer child to me now.

@wild_wildwest2000, 1 June

THE NEW COMMUTE

Commute was a pain today.
I stepped barefoot onto a piece of Lego

@jestersbauble, 30 March

Left work at 5.30. Home with kids at 5.31.
God I miss the commute.

@martymcfyonthewall, 6 June

On the way to work today, I barely managed to evade Officer "Poo-poo head" in a high-speed chase up the stairs.

@cccork693, 3 May

'Daddy I made you coffee' sounds so sweet, doesn't it? Right until that point when you realise he made it with Bisto and stirred it with his toothbrush.

@terryhenry312, 18 May

Silently crept up to the office attic on tiptoes, holding my breath. Open the door and close it behind me without a sound. Relief, joy and victory all etched on my face.

Then my six year old swings round on my swivelly chair like Blofeld. 'SURPRISE, DADDY FACE!'

@noble_ali, 29 March

6 weeks into lockdown. Sometimes I just go and stand in the bath holding the shower rail. Makes me feel like I'm on the Tube. Rush-hour mayhem stuck under a sweaty armpit never seemed sweeter.

@hedwigfliesagain, 8 June

DADS OFFICE
DAD IS CURRENTLY UNAVAILABLE Please CONTACT MOM
OR The Answer To YOUR QUESTION IS:
(1) IN THE WASH
(2) Have a piece OF FRUIT instead
(3) Be NICE To YOUR SISTER
(4) Be NICE To YOUR BROTHER
(5) NO!!
BY

Put on a shirt and tie today. Kid asked my wife "who that man is".

@bringmesunchyme, 14 April

Here's my new pre-work ritual that has replaced the commute:

7am Casio alarm wakes me up. Suddenly filled with hatred for the reliable watch manufacturer.

7.15am Carry child downstairs, both he and I wearing the same expression that says "Why am I awake, you f***er?

7.30am Feed baby. Search "Mr Tumble" on BBC iPlayer. They've got 30 episodes. Praise the Lord! Make mistake of singing along to theme tune. Baby now cries when I don't do that for the next episode.

8.30am Starting to worry that my baby sees me as an underwhelming Mr Tumble substitute

9am Baby down for nap. Open work email on laptop.

9.15am Close work email. Watch YouTube video about learning how to juggle. F**k you, Tumble. I shall defeat you.

@babygotback1982, 7 May

Never realised how much I missed sitting down, not making eye contact with anyone and not talking for an hour and a half.

@mrs_robins0n, 28 March

SEND HELP

BOSS: due to the virus we need everybody to work from home.
ME: please, I have a family.

@TheCatWhisprer, 11 March

Another tough day's work come and gone. I'll celebrate by changing out of last night's pyjamas and into... tonight's pyjamas.

@440_apollo, 26 March

Pretty sure my boy is
sat outside my study door
maliciously farting through
the gap.

@thisissparta, 28 March

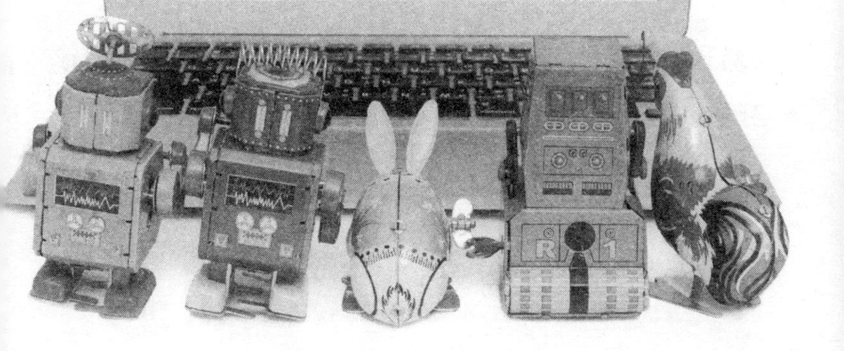

My 6 yr old has been watching Monty Python and has now started screaming: "I fart in your general erection". I'm not sure where to go from here.

@slings_andarras, 29 April

So in a major fail today, my 5 year old worked out how to add things to our Alexa shopping list. Let's just say a unicorn duvet cover and 10 packs of hundreds and thousands are on their way.

@deano_barry, 30 March

My 5 yr old has hidden my car keys and has made several demands if I want to see them again. I won't negotiate with terrorists.

Update: I am now in possession of my car keys, which I'm now using to "buy a lot of sweets" as per the terms of the ransom.

@DaddyOGodno, 23 May

My kid is so fed up with me working from home that he left a banana skin at the top of the stairs. I'm afraid.

@wild_wildwest2000, 23 May

Dissertation word count added to today: 0
Ears sewn back on soft toys: 2
Piles of dog barf cleaned up: 5
Tantrums (children): 2
Tantrums (self): 3
Bossin' lockdown.

@LouiseHhorniman, 18 April

Found a note slid under the door to my study written in red crayon. It read "I know you're in there". Reminded me of Sideshow Bob's letters to Bart in *The Simpsons.*

@aspihall17, 6 May

VIDEO CALL
LIVE
WORK

Opened my study door to find a note stuck onto it and an empty plate outside. Note (from 4 year old) reads: "Daddy I made you lunch. But I eated it."

@curtiscounihan, 8 June

6 yr old: "Daddy, what's the difference between being locked down and being locked up."

Me: In prison, people give you food, you can get work done and you can sleep for 8 hours.

@carmanchameleon, 20 March

Found a toy horse's head on my pillow during my WFH lunchbreak. Worried my daughter has been watching *The Godfather*.

@marcus_levy, 17 May

Me *pounding on the bathroom door*: Let me in, I need to brush my teeth!
8 yr old: Mom. You're just going on a Zoom call, nobody can smell your breath.

@JeninLdnont, 17 June

5 yr old daughter: "Daddy if I hurt you then you don't have to work today".

@antonWilshere, 8 April

WINNING

My working day today with a 9-month-old:
9.15–9.45
11.45–12
12–12.05
12.30–11.05
4.30–5.05
6.55–7.10
Bossing this WFH shizzle.

@sarah_chantelle_44, 2 April

Made this today and stuck it on my study door at 9 am.

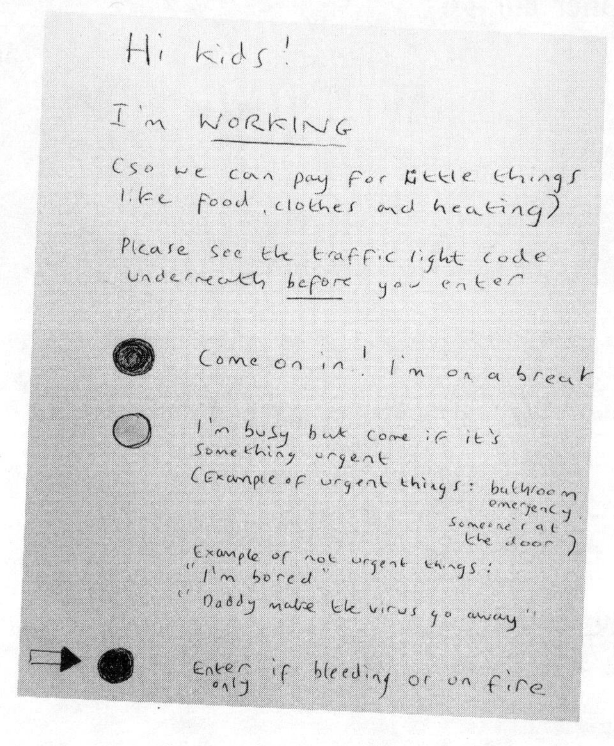

Thought I was a genius. Then at 9.45, there was a hammering at my door.

4 year old: 'Daddy it's a mergency – my unicorn looks sad.' #wfhfail

@roger_johndunley, 1 May

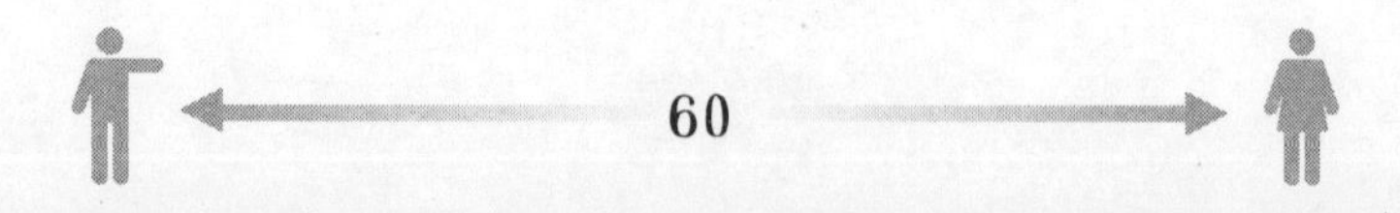

Giving your three year old an ice cream for breakfast's fine during lockdown, right? Anyone? Bueller?

@mack_the_knife, 2 April

Left my phone unattended and kid managed to get Siri to call Ian (my boss) and ask for the day off. I now have the day off.

@daddydaycare97, 5 June

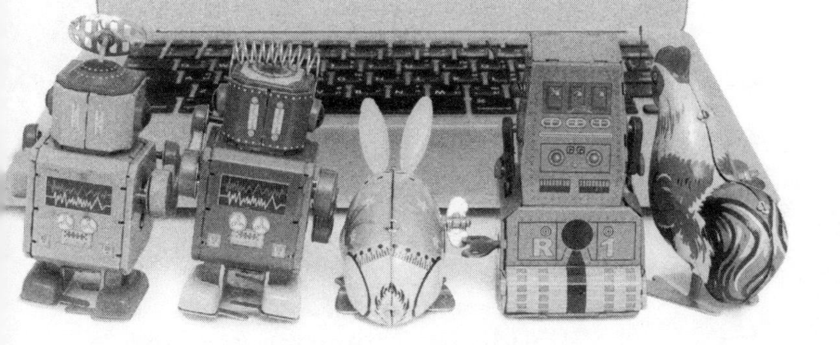

I ♡ MY DOGS
ROCKY
MILLY
BY DEREK
FAMILY

"Stages of working from home:

Monday: Hooray! I get to stay at home and see my kids more during the day.
Tuesday: Please send me as many urgent emails and tasks as possible. I'll do all the work. Evenings/weekends not a problem."

@louloulou10, 29 March

"My five year old made me this bowtie today to "make my smelly t-shirt look smarter on Zoomed".

@bohnasrho, 20 April

CHAPTER 3

Kitchen Nightmares

SO THE FORTUNATE few who have managed to find flour, sugar and eggs in the supermarkets have been charitably ballsing up their bakes for the amusement of everyone else. Maybe our brains just aren't in the right place at the moment.

We normally live with our adorable mini wrecking balls laying waste to our kitchens on a daily basis, but add quarantine to the mix and those same kitchens are witnessing even more ludicrous conversations, outrageous negotiations and high-quality cock-ups. You know what, though – us parents are pulling through. And maybe we'll all bond over this in the future (i.e. hold each other while we cry), showing off our battle scars (i.e. comparing how much we spent on family therapy) and talking wistfully of the day that we joined together in spirit to defeat a common enemy.

In this chapter, you'll find domestic tales of banana bread fails, some epic truth-bending, parents and kids whose brains have left the building, and every child's favourite subject (poo, for the non-parents among you). In other chapters, some parents have managed to battle through against the odds and record wins. Not here. This is an unqualified shambles.

CULINARY COCK-UPS

Run out of spaghetti so had to use the novelty penis-shaped pasta I got given on my hen-do. "Why is the pasta in funny shapes?" my son asks.
Panicking "We... er... got them on a camping trip. They're tent-shaped."

@chrissy11walton, 23 May

My banana bread rose in the oven then let out an audible sigh and imploded spectacularly. If that doesn't mirror lockdown in general I don't know what does.

@marciathomas, 14 June

Me: Banana bread's been in the oven for 20 mins, so far so good.
4yo: I finished mashing the bananas Mummy. Can I put them in the pan?
Me: D'oh!

@sparkly_sarah, 17 April

Let kids decorate the cupcakes. Ratio of actual cake to sprinkles: 1:100

@fairy_dust, 4 June

Didn't think this needed spelling out, but no, Lego does not magically become edible if you decorate your cupcake with it.

@paule11liot, 1 May

My daughter just put two Mr Bump plasters on my cake to help "mend its breaky bits"

@parkourSusie, 3 June

I'm not sure if you've
ever slipped on a banana skin
before but nothing quite prepares
you for that unique mixture of
embarrassment and surprise.
Fortunately my 12 year old son
saw what happened...
and stepped over me on the
way to the fridge.
@Katycgoldstein, 6 April

There are only so many times I can keep telling my 4 year old you can't bake poo until I give in and make a turd traybake.

@marinawright1980, 17 June

First attempt at baking today. Fire alarm went off and my cookies are not social distancing at all.

@ed_wrightdavies, 22 May

There's no easy way to say this, but the sourdough loaf I baked seems to have acquired a penis. I made it some long flappy ears to make it look like an elephant, but well they just ended up looking like balls so I guess I'll just cash in my parenting chips.

@fairy_dust, 16 June

So we used to have:
If you're naughty, Santa won't leave you any presents.
If you're naughty, the tooth fairy won't visit.

Now we've got: if you're naughty, mom will bake you another cookie.

@TonyRFM, 8 June

Me: Do you like the bread?
6yo: Mummy it tastes like feet.
Me: Please clarify whether that's good or bad.

@yvettemcmahon, 2 May

I'd love to tell you that I didn't have to Google the colours of the rainbow in order to decorate my rainbow cookies. Ain't happening tho.

@fairy_dust, 19 April

After we put the kids to bed, I whipped up a Nutella cake.
Well, Nutella on three bits of bread sandwiched together. That counts, right?

@jojo_eames, 18 July

We're out of toilet paper but we've still got flour so I'm baking bog roll shaped bread instead for posterity.

@deb0rara, 23 April

Making pizzas and, despite my warnings, my toddler just put so many toppings on it that the dough sagged like a 40-year-old testicle.

@madbaddad, 15 April

My 10 year old told me my cookies look like Voldemort's face at the end of Harry Potter 1. She's not wrong.

@patel_anupJ, 16 April

Mum: Who's eaten the rainbow sprinkles for the cupcakes?
5 year old: I don't know.
3 year old: *Spitting out sprinkles* DADDY!

@PhoebeRWallis, 24 March

"Mama can we make poo-cake?"

@hannyvanarkel, 20 May

UNPRECEDENTED SCENES

Before quarantine: No! Cookies are not an acceptable breakfast.
Now: Yo, how many cookies do you want for breakfast today?

@saltymamas, 21 May

Right kids, it's pesto sardines on an amaretto biscuit again tonight.

@DaveTWifgall, 27 April

Pretty sure my 7 year old just said 'quarter pounder with fries, please' in his sleep.

@andy_robinson2, 15 May

Just found my 7 year old son pouring milk directly into a cereal packet.
grabs spoon

@andy_robinson2, 5 May

Just poured anti-bac instead of olive oil on the salad. Brain has finally checked out.

@NellYMoran, 28 May

During lockdown, part of me has started to believe that repeatedly opening and closing the door of the fridge will make food magically appear.

@alex_ryback23, 27 April

Before lockdown:
3.5 year old: Mummy, can I lick the bowl?
Me: Sure, sweetie!

During lockdown:
3.5 year old: Mummy, can I lick the bowl?
Me: (Don't tell your child to f**k off, don't tell your child to f**k off)

@Andrea_Susini99, 30 March

My husband has been making pancakes and eggs for breakfast every morning and my kids are becoming accustomed to a standard I am not prepared to maintain after he returns to work.

@AnecdtlBrthCtrl, 25 March

DAD, when are we going to put the Bananas in?

My kids have been experimenting with a new diet called, "if you snack all day long, there's really no need for meals" and honestly, same.

@SnarkyMommy78, 23 April

TBH, if any of the Fat, Sugars or Salt content on food packaging are highlighted in green, they can get the fuck out of my kitchen.

@braindad, 16 May

Me: what do you want for dinner?
3yo: nothing.
Me: you want cheese on that nothing?
3yo: yes please.

@daddydoubts, 21 May

Just been rumbled at midnight dipping my whole hand in a secretly stashed jar of Nutella. Honestly think my wife would have been happier if she'd caught me with my nob in a hooker.

@needlenose_ned, 22 June

Used up the last can of John West tuna from the back of the cupboard for the kids' supper. Looks like hubby and I will be enjoying malt vinegar chasers with a stale taco shell entrée to follow tonight.

@KarenTCowdray, 3 April

YUP, THAT SOUNDS ABOUT RIGHT

5yo has created a race track in the kitchen. You're now only allowed to enter if you make a noise like a Formula One car. You know, kids generally talk a lot of shit, but not this time. I'm in.

@ewanburroughs, 10 June

On the bright side, this quarantine has brought my thighs closer together.

@SnarkyMommy78, 26 April

Mummy, I'll help you with the shopping list.

@EmmaSTennant, 4 August

Mum: As a treat we're
going to have takeaway tonight.
What would you like?
6 yo: Pizza!
8 yo: Two pizzas!
4 yo: Clown fish!
Dad: You know Nemo's a
clownfish, right?

Today's edition of meltdown has been
brought to you by dad.
@madhousemax, 29 June

WILL TRADE HUSBAND FOR BAKING POWDER!

@Sophiesnowflake, 4 April

Teddy bear's picnic in the kitchen. 6yo has made them wear paper towel masks and placed them two metres apart. I can't tell if this is adorable or devastating.

@Tom1Grange, 15 June

Today's high jinks have involved wearing thick socks and seeing who can slide furthest across the kitchen. 7 year old declared the winner and celebrates 'an epic win' by pulling his shirt over his head and running straight into 5 year old at speed, who slides across the floor on his bum.
Dad: We have a new winner!
Just your average lockdown lunch hour.

@OrlaYoungman, 28 May

We've got four tomato plants growing in the kitchen for each member of the family and, well the cat managed to shit in our youngest child's plant pot. Youngest's now "on strike". Not quite sure what that entails, but it sounds good!

@braindad, 10 May

Kids During The Regular School Year: Take a single corner bite of their sandwich and eat exactly three raisins.

Kids During Quarantine: Shovel food into their mouths like they're in a hot dog eating contest trying to win an 8 million dollar prize.

@gfishandnuggets, 9 April

Here's my shopping list on the week before lockdown and four weeks later.

@Jess_reynolds1981, 27 April

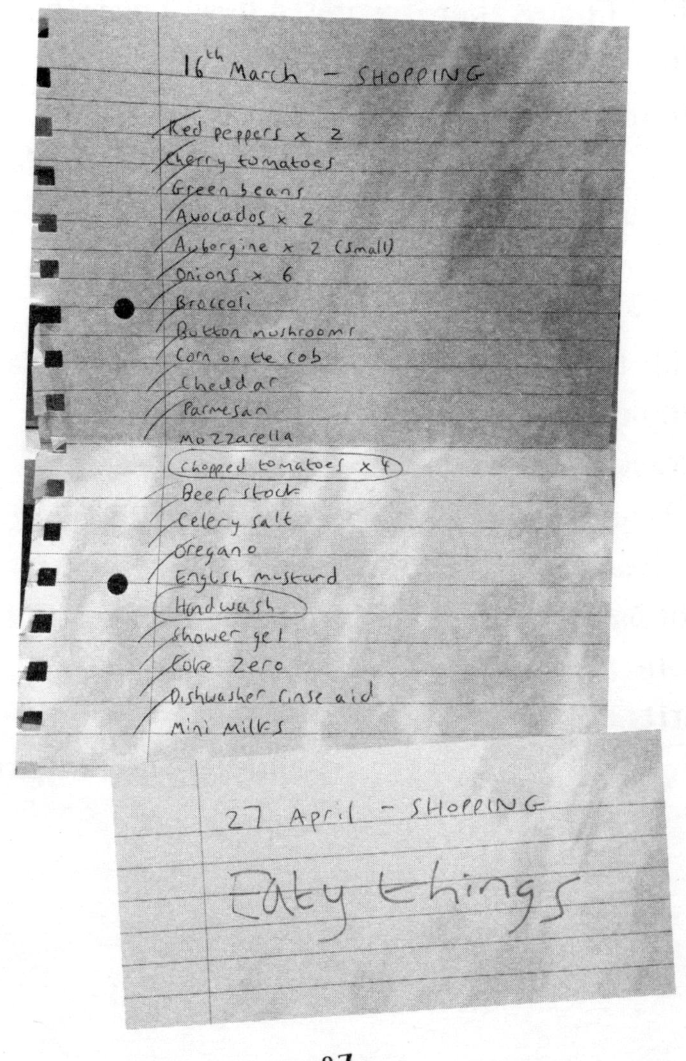

16th March – SHOPPING

Red peppers x 2
Cherry tomatoes
Green beans
Avocados x 2
Aubergine x 2 (small)
Onions x 6
Broccoli
Button mushrooms
Corn on the cob
Cheddar
Parmesan
Mozzarella
Chopped tomatoes x 4
Beef stock
Celery salt
Oregano
English mustard
Handwash
Shower gel
Coke Zero
Dishwasher rinse aid
Mini Milks

27 April – SHOPPING

Eaty things

Anyone else buy bananas and deliberately watch them go brown, refuse to let kids have them for no good reason then say:
"Well I guess there's nothing for it but make banana bread."
Me neither.

@PhoebeRWallis, 13 May

This is what our house has become:
9 year old: Can I have a donut?
Me: No!
9 year old: But I always had one at 11 o clock at real school. I think I've got withdrawal.
Husband (mumbling): Cold turkey, eh. Tough.
9 year old (yelling): I don't want cold turkey!!!!

@chrissy_yeo, 9 May

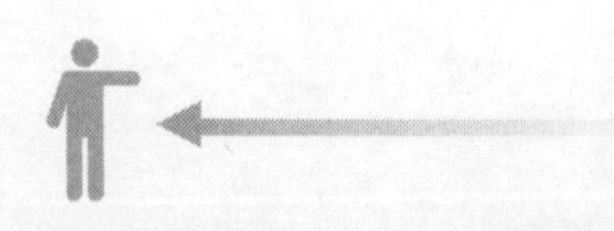

BY ROISIN
BY TERESA
CHOC
MARK
CHOC

Just made mince pies while singing Christmas carols. It's June 21.

@ionatalbot1, 21 June

Kids have coloured in the flooring in the kitchen to make cooking a bit more high-octane. There's now a lava pit, a bog of eternal stench and kids only VIP section that I'm not allowed in.

@ed_mckinleyR, 3 July

My husband and I have birthdays two days apart. We both bought each other a cheese knife. I'm glad we're both investing in our new lockdown profession.

@EvaHoughton, 1 June

It's got to 6pm and no one's had a tantrum yet today. The quiet is making me uncomfortable. I think I'm gonna have to step up.

"Sorry kids we've only got Marmite peanut butter left for dinner." That oughta do it.

@DanJBrowne, 20 May

CHAPTER 4

Healthy Body, Healthy Mind

PEOPLE HAVE GONE one of two ways in lockdown. Some fu**ers have taken up running or cycling or joined online fitness apps, while most parents have taken up professional snacking. Our creativity and resourcefulness have really come to the fore, as we invent new mealtimes and throw together cocktails from questionable liquors given as favours at weddings. That's what we do for kicks these days, along with thrill-seeking excursions to take the bins out or sharpening our rally car-style pram skills to avoid people on the pavement.

In our ever-broadening CVs, in addition to our new roles as teachers, parents have also become emergency hairdressers, and lo, the coronacut was christened. It's quite an achievement making a five-year-old look like Yoda with just five minutes and a pair of clippers. And yet, this is one thing most parents are bossing.

While "mastering" these new skills and navigating the new normal, we're all flirting with madness on a daily basis, but the important thing to remember is that it's all going to be fine. *Keeps repeating sentence while rocking back and forth.*

THE NEW NORMAL

7 year old: "Mummy, why does our doorstep say 'welcome' on it?"
Me: "I don't know anymore."

@LouiseC3000, 19 April

Low point of lockdown so far:
Five-year-old: "I decorated your mask, Daddy, to let people know that you're frowning underneath it."

@sam_durrance, 4 July

Left the house for the first time in a week to take the bin out. Feeling like quite the adrenaline junkie.

@ZoeTC001, 31 May

Kid just drew a picture of a coronavirus particle hugging another one. Underneath she wrote
"Looks like FUN".

@joeydonnas_gal, 17 May

I love you Mummy. But I think I love the iPad more.

@wendy_smith1975, 30 March

Took the bins out wearing a mask, a bike helmet, a pair of gloves and some disposable shoe covers. Ain't no virus gonna ruin my jam. Look down and barefoot 4 year old is behind me carrying the little recycling bin.
"I help Daddy."
"That's so sweet of you son" (Internal thought: you'll be the death of me).

@jonnyrico33, 7 June

My kids have entered the "let's sing Christmas songs all day" phase of quarantine. Please send thoughts and prayers. Or noise cancelling headphones.

@saltymamas, 20 May

Our first trip outside the house definitely wasn't scarring.

@oscarjfm, 19 July

Daughter's favourite colouring pencil broke in half and I'm now treating the wound with savlon and a plaster. Maybe it's just lockdown but this all feels perfectly sensible to me.

@roflrolf7, 22 June

Can't find the page in the parenting book that tells you what to do when your child walks towards you carrying their own faeces.

In fairness, we have no toilet roll. I'll probably be doing the same thing shortly.

@75BrenchleyG, 31 May

it's
5 o'clock
somewhere

In case you're feeling concerned about your kid's screen time, just know that we reached the screen time overload portion of quarantine where my 4yo asked me if I could "turn off the sun for a few minutes" because it was too bright on his eyes.

@gfishandnuggets, 16 April

Highs and lows of lockdown so far: Me (encouragingly): If you're happy and you know it, clap your hands!

5 year old: I'm not happy daddy. I don't think I ever will be again.

Mum: Pancakes are ready

5 year old: YAYYYYYYYYYYYYYYYYYYYYYYYYY!!!!!!!!!!!

@aaron_hughes33, 28 April

I can hear a child screaming. Oh wait, it's not one of mine!

Probably shouldn't have shouted "In your face, sucker" out of the open attic window tho.

@robert_vanburgh5, 5 July

The highlight of my day is pretend-going to the toilet to get five minutes peace. Here's a conversation I just overheard going on outside the toilet door.

5 year old: I think mummy's losted her bottom.
4 year old: Maybe it got flusht way.

@beckyb533, 15 April

Conversation starter after putting kids to bed:

If you had to do without one of them, would it be sex or takeaways?
(said quicker than a particle in the Large Hadron Collider): Sex

@StuartJHardy, 14 June

8: I made up an imaginary place where I'm the king and I have lots of servants.
Me: Am I one of the servants in your imaginary place?
8: No Mummy you're my servant in real life.

@mumInbits, 24 July

SLIPPING STANDARDS

"Do we have to go for another walk, Dad? I mean, I've already walked upstairs twice today."

@dadontheedge_99, 28 April

Poured gin into an empty water bottle earlier. No one will be the wiser.
11 am (yelling from somewhere upstairs): "Mummy, this water tastes funny."

@ma_toldyouno, 20 May

It's amazing how quarantine with kids has lowered my standards for cleanliness. Like, a lot. I've gone from "Please, kids, try not to make a mess," to "I don't care if you bathe outside in glitter slime and sand, as long as it buys me an hour of time."

@gfishandnuggets, 24 May

It's like pulling teeth trying to get my 4yo to regularly wash his hands, but he absolutely won't share his chocolate chip ice cream with his sister because of "Corona Birus Germs," so now I'm quite confident that this kid has a bright future in sales or politics.

@gfishandnuggets, 30 July

ALL BEER
SOLD OUT

My 3yo just reminded ME to wash my hands after we got home so if anything good were to come out of this pandemic it's that we're raising a less gross genera– ok never mind he just ate a booger.

@daddydoubts, 6 June

Smart alek 8 year old this morning: "The tooth fairy didn't show up last night. Must be a non-essential worker."

@alikrauss1990, 5 May

Me: What day is it?
My wife: It's...Wednesday?
Our oldest: [who has recently learned the days of the week] No, it's Tuesday.
My wife and I: [simultaneous whisper] f**king nerd.

@HomeWithPeanut, 14 April

I miss interacting with people that I'm not legally obligated to interact with.

@SnarkyMommy78, 30 April

Is it ok to tell your kids that the virus spreads to people who talk too loudly? Happy to pay the therapy bill in ten years.

@cheryl_tweety, 4 May

I've managed to develop RSI in my wrist and I'm putting it down to the weird windmill wave I now do on every bloody Zoom call with the family.

@rorydurrant1, 29 May

Mr CJ: Make sure the baby doesn't try to lick the cat's bottom.
Mrs CJ: I'm on it, just after I take this photo.

@nathanejoyce, 18 July

This morning I found our 3 year old eating cereal from a wine glass. That's a developmental milestone right?

@threetimedaddy, 17 May

I gave the kids a big amazon box to play with and they all climbed inside and seemed happy so I taped up the box and returned it to amazon I'm sure they're fine

@muminbits, 25 May

I'm fairly sure that my 4 year old thinks that his grandparents live in a window on my laptop.

@kumar_nikesh, 18 May

Is it ok to tell your kids that the virus spreads to people who talk too loudly? Happy to pay the therapy bill in ten years.

@cheryl_tweety, 4 May

Had quite a job explaining to my 5 year old that the reason there's no money under the pillow is because the tooth fairy is also social distancing.

@philf1ddler, 22 April

SELF-CARE

Weekly Screen Time Report: u ok bro?

@daddydoubts, 26 April

I've bought everything we could possibly need to survive lockdown. We won't need to leave the house for weeks.
(Later that day) "Just popping out to get a Snickers".

@mumtastic, 2 April

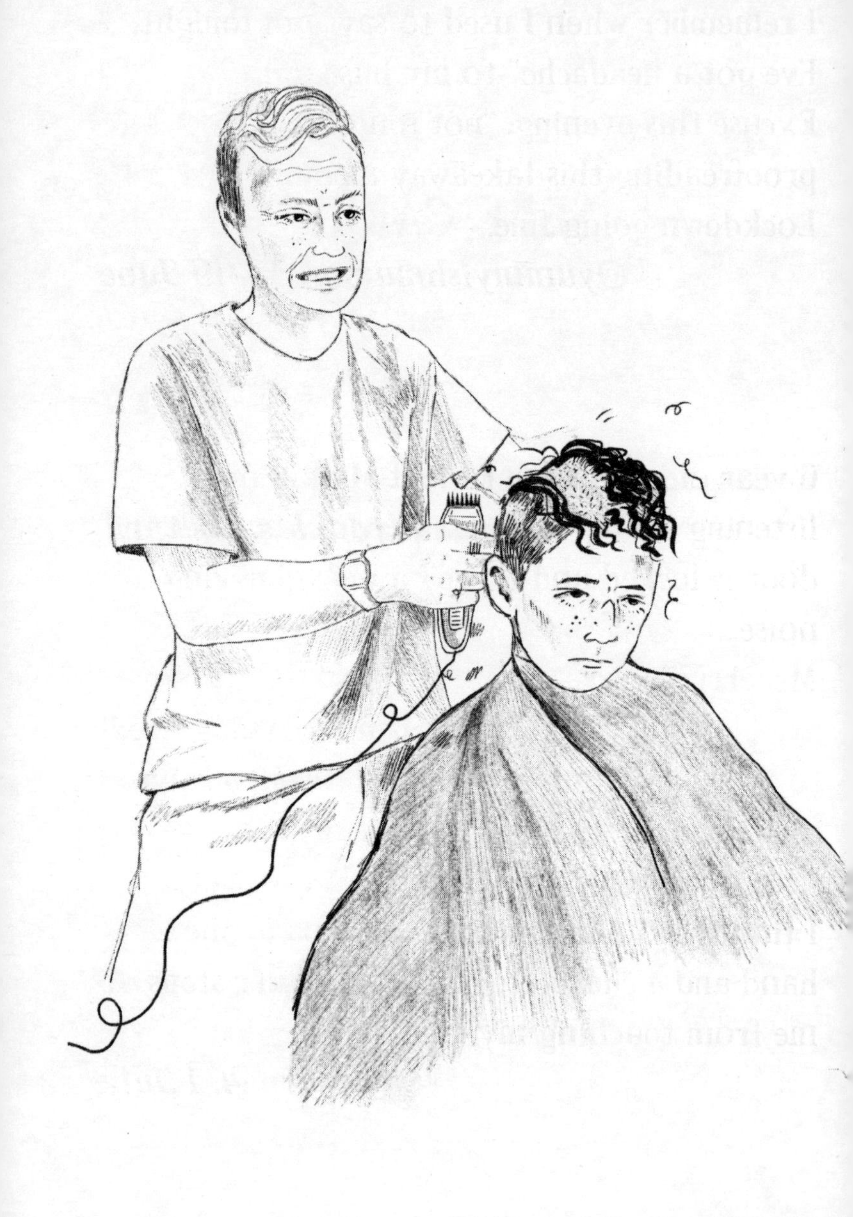

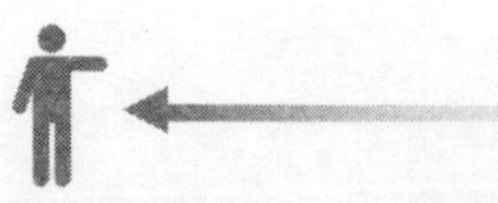

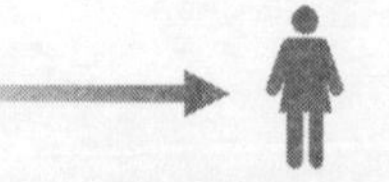

I remember when I used to say "not tonight, I've got a headache" to my husband. Excuse this evening: "not tonight – I'm proofreading this takeaway menu." Lockdown going fine.

@yummyishmummy33, 19 June

6 year old: I just heard that Mummy's listening to Joe Wicks in the bedroom but the door is locked and there's a weird buzzing noise.

Me: errrrrrrrr

@georgeharris, 16 April

I find that holding a glass of wine in one hand and a chocolate bar in the other stops me from touching my face.

@geo_p0pe4, 1 July

So face masks are compulsory in shops from today. To be on the safe side, I've told my kids they need to keep their mouth covered at home as well.

@Threetimedaddy, 24 July

My biggest lockdown fail? Dislocating my shoulder while applauding over-enthusiastically during the Thursday NHS clap. Had to go to A&E. Receptionist told me "Your heart's in the right place. Not sure your brain is."

@daniellyons_1, 3 May

The haircut went ok. Photo on right taken after left ear was reattached.

@Daxwhatboy, 15 May

How hairdressers manage to both talk and not cut people's ears off I don't f***ing know.

@WTFpar3nt, 29 May

Cut my daughter's hair today. I can almost hear the therapist asking her when the self-loathing began.

@wanderingWinter, 11 May

CHAPTER 5

Musings

SO WE'VE STARTED to see the light at the end of the tunnel, although, because most of us haven't been outside in a while, that normally uplifting mental image is surprisingly frightening.

I think we can all agree that it's felt like a rollercoaster so far – downs, ups, hearts racing, kids puking and moments where you feel like maybe the folks in charge have no clue what they're doing. Unlike a rollercoaster, though, something tells me that the chorus of "Again, again!" won't be reverberating through the enclosure.

These tweets have a more reflective note, like that moment of sobriety when you find yourself in a questionable takeaway at 2 a.m. and start to question your life choices.

Which is probably about the time that most of these tweets were written. It's for that reason that they're my favourites. Comedy laced with a sprinkling of tragedy.

I don't like to brag but I had 19 seconds earlier where none of my kids yelled, cried, peed on the floor or asked if we can adopt a pigeon and call it Peppa
@MumInBits, 21 July

Things I've learned during lockdown, number 77.

If I didn't have a child to dress every day, I think I would have forgotten how to put on a pair of trousers by now.

@therealjimhacker, 28 June

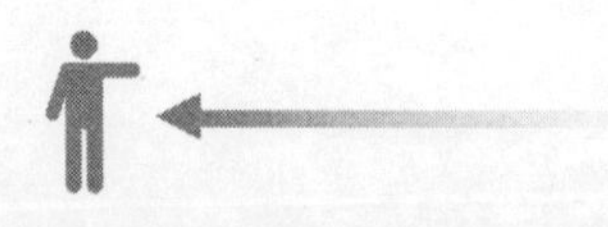

For future lockdowns, anyone know how I can create a looping video of me sitting at my desk to play during Zoom meetings like that bit in *Speed* where Keanu fools Dennis Hopper?

@wild_wildwest2000, 9 June

To those of you who still feel like you're superior, remember this; after this pandemic is over we will all have the skill level of a toddler when it comes to dressing ourselves.

@HomewithPeanut, 18 May

How's lockdown affected my parenting? Well, I've discovered a level of fatigue beyond 'can't be arsed'.

@IanThomas01, 11 May

My dear little girl is two & I hope twos won't be too terrible for her, but this week she cried about a bogey in her nose, then cried when I took it out & didn't give it back, then cried cos sky is too blue, then cried poking herself in eye doing head, shoulders, knees & toes.

@EmmaSTennant, 23 July

So me and the 3 year old tried to paint the message "Thank you Heroes" today.
It came out "Thank you Hoes". I mean I'm still putting it in the window. Girl's gotta eat.

@nancynmyers, 7 May

Managed to get an hour's peace by introducing my 4 year old to a pair of binoculars and asking him to keep a look out for the virus. I suggest you all do the same.

@Nick_Wickremasinghe, 29 June

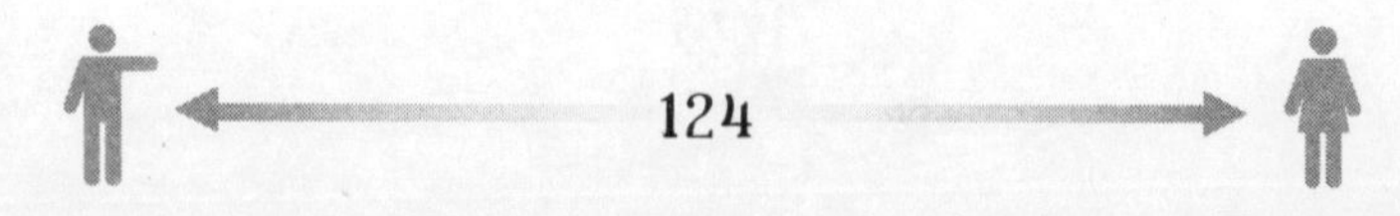

We don't run our house with a strict schedule but we do naturally fall into a routine, for example mid-morning is when we all go into separate rooms to cry.

@daddydoubts, 9 April

Nursery reopened today and I may have accidentally celebrated it in front of my kids like when Liverpool won the Champions League.

@Vinny_Mansour, 1 June

6 yo: I'm bored of Harry Potter.
Me: Wait, what?! That's not in the manual. I...er... "Stupefy!" (waving chopstick like magic wand).

@JKM619, 7 July

In our house, we've started doing our own government daily briefings, and to be frank, they make a lot more f***ing sense.

@harvey_monster, 20 June

Parenting during lockdown:
10% distraction
10% education
20% bribery
25% threats
40% TV

@clemmieCstewart, 19 June

As a parent, I shall mostly remember watching Stanley Tucci's Negroni video in slow motion and thinking "that sounds like a lovely way to make a drink" while downing a vat of wine.

@nicolaegham99, 30 July

What's the first thing you want to do when lockdown's over?
4yo: Watch *Peppa Pig*!
Me: Er......

@DrAMosley, 6 August

Definitely feel closer to my children now and we've spent much more time as a family.

Just not sure if either of those things are positive.

@jamielyons1988, 17 July

During lockdown, I've specialised in sneaking empty bottles of booze into other people's glass recycling boxes. So after lockdown, I'm retraining as a motherfucking ninja.

@Debs_surfs, 19 July

Looking back on lockdown, I'm glad I really threw myself into keeping fit. The eight muscles in my jaw are in bloody tip-top condition.

@LouiseHhorniman, 30 June

Lego pieces swallowed: 2
Broken bones: 1
Trips to A&E: 2
Tantrums: 1,356

That's just me, though.
The kids are fine.

@EdWiseman, 31 July

Wondering how many people in my neighbourhood are going to call the same babysitter after lockdown's over. Shall I send her some cash in advance as a bribe?

@k00kykaty, 1 August

Just made the mistake of looking at my step count this morning for the first time during lockdown. It may as well have said "heart attack imminent".

@liamosullivan99, 21 July

Best not to look at your website history during the lockdown period. It turns out that after losing my job I've become a professional masturbator.

@bringmesunchyme, 18 July

Daddy approval ratings are in. The question posed was: how happy are you that Daddy's home all the time?
Wife: 23%
6 year old kid: 80%
13 year old kid: 37%
Dog: 100%

@terryhenry312, 16 July

"Amaia's little coronavirus" (with blusher).

@westhoveactually, 29 May

Got to see a lot more of our hometown during lockdown: the parks, the fields. And we've made the collective decision as a family that it's shit where we live and we're moving.

@ThomPhillips, 22 July

Sat down as a family to try and record the best film trailer complete with intense voiceover. The winner (our 12 year old):

"In a world unlike any other, the public respond well to a scientist's advice and go about their business calmly."

I'd pay to see that.

@johnrlongfellow, 29 July

Every household: How are we all going to cope when we have to come up with plausible excuses again for not seeing each other's family?

@liamosullivan99, 2 July

My kid went to after
school club on the 23rd March.
Haven't heard from
her since. I'm sure she's ok.
@aspihall17, 30 May

"Is a person who works with keys a key
working key worker?"
Wooooaaaaah – that's too clever for me.
My brain cells are marinating in vodka.

@donrwaters, 2 August

My kids were completely silent for about 5 seconds today and to be honest it felt better than any sex I've had in years. And longer.

@threetimedaddy, 29 July

Dog just licked six month old's face clean after a fairly disastrous attempt at weaning. Dog is delighted. Kid is delighted. Three year old who watched the whole thing is delighted. I'm going with the majority.

@andyscott_1990, 20 July

Can we get away with saying that Santa's only given you two stocking gifts this year because presents have to socially distance like everyone else?

@DrAMosley, 6 August

LOOK DADDY, I'M WASHING THE SHOPPING

Dad: Draw your favourite thing on TV!
Kid draws Netflix logo
We're coping fine.

@joeydonnas_gal, 17 May

Now I'm not proud of it but I did teach my 4 year old son today that you can blow out birthday candles with a fart.

@Vinny_Mansour, 1 June

So what have we learned? When families spend more time together, the divorce rate goes up. When lockdown's over, I'm moving to Tahiti. And I'm doing it for YOU GUYS. You're welcome.

@rodrigomontoya2, 5 July

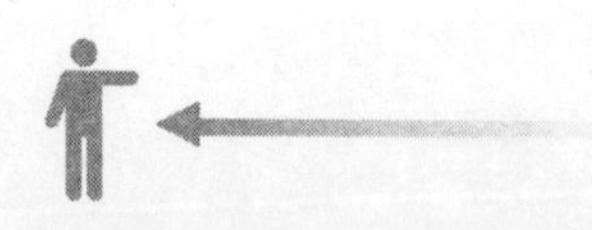

"Daddy I made my own PPE with Sellotape."

@harveymonster, 7 August

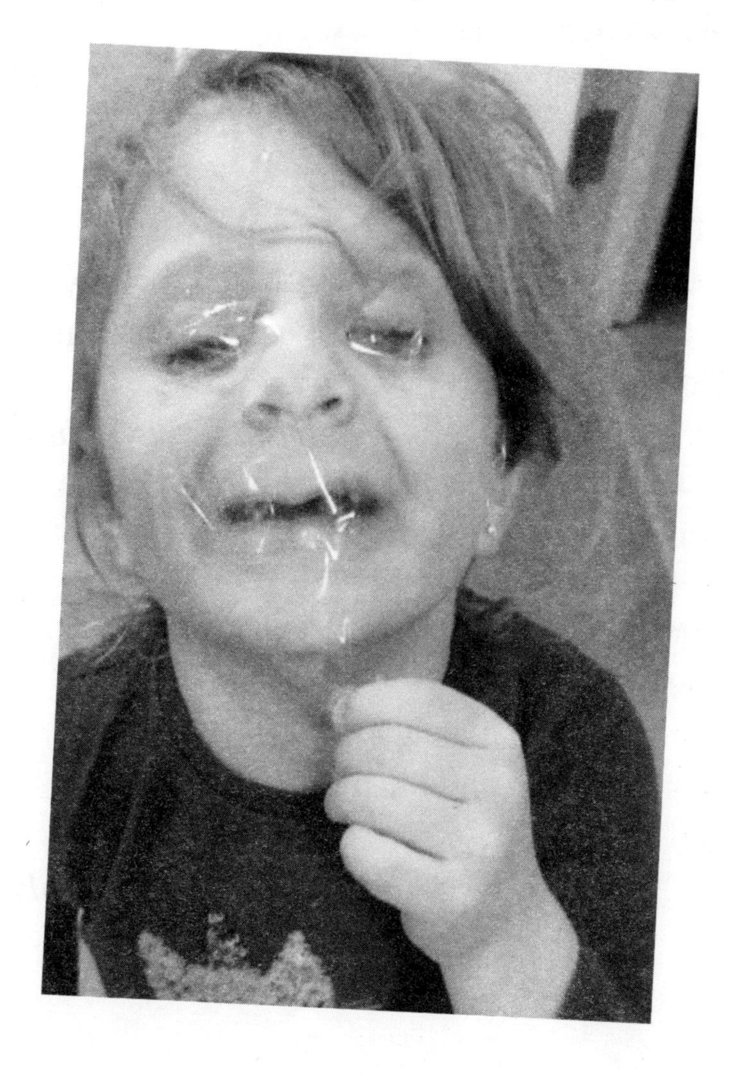

Me: Did you just Facetime each other from the same room?
13 year old: Er, yeah. I wanted her to pass the remote
Me:

I think we've reached the peak.

@mrremountjoy, 16 April

Kid's rainbow drawing was beautiful. Haven't got the heart to tell him that the pot of gold on the right and the two clouds on the left just make it look like a cock and balls though.

@moreno_juan, 16 May

Been pondering the big questions today like at what point is my kids' sharting accidental and at what point does it turn into malice afore-thought.

Pandemic Protest Poo

@nickywright1984, 17 July

Just briefly forgot one of my kid's names but it's cool, no one will ever find out so as long as I don't post it on Twitter.

Sorry – my social filter fucked off on March 23rd.

@number9WT, 30 July

The below reads: Ana (Mummy) is the moost eevilist villin.
Already framed on the wall as a lockdown memento. With one slight embellishment: a superhero cape.

@allamasm, 14 May

What a lovely day it is, kids. Get the fuck in the garden.

@haisha99, 19 July

Best memory of lockdown? Locking ourselves out during the clap for carers and forming a human pyramid to reach the first floor window. We're practically The Incredibles.

@EdDFloyd, 6 August

"Come get your children" and all the other text messages I never thought I'd receive from someone downstairs.

@Stonecolddad316, 4 May

If you haven't stared out of the window and imagined yourself in a private jet, with no kids, destroying all-you-can-eat bread sticks, whilst cancelling plans like it's 2019, then you're quarantining wrong.

@Stonecolddad316, 20 April

My idea about practicing times tables sparked a meltdown and now I'm trapped in a power struggle and the morning is ruined and the pancakes are cold and I wish I would've stayed quiet and let him keep watching *Teen Titans.*

@JeninLdnont, 6 August

mom's wine
DAD's GIN
BREAKING NEWS
SCHOOLS TO
REOPEN SOON

Here's me trying to compile this book. I'm the one with the headphones but this goofy bastard keeps distracting me.

@nathanejoyce, 7 August

Acknowledgements

First, a huge thank you to my wife and best friend Tarah for her support, patience and all-round awesomeness. And to little Mr Finn, who I've shamelessly exploited for the sake of comedy photographs. And I can't put together a book without mentioning Zsófia and Laurie. Strong showing.

To Oliver Holden-Rea. I've watched you degenerate (further) into a shambles during lockdown, but you're a glorious human. And *hates to admit it* really good at your job.

A big thank you to another Oliver in my life, Dr Oliver Harvey. A genuine hero. And to Ana, Amaia, Clara and Xabi – the stars of Chapter 5.
Massive thanks to Helen and Dax Ginn and Chip and Hester. Legends – every one of you.

Oscar Mathew, Jake Armstrong, Donal Coonan and Roger John Dunley for ongoing comic relief. Thank you also to Ben Dunn, Emma Tennant (and Constance!) and Rachel Bridgewater, to Alex Allden and Katie Meegan at Welbeck for your Grade A work and to the fantastic Emma Scully for the illustrations.

And then, there are the stars of Parent Twitter, without whom this book would not have happened. You rock! I'd like to thank the following in particular for letting me raid their Twitter feeds:

@muminbits,
@threetimedaddy,

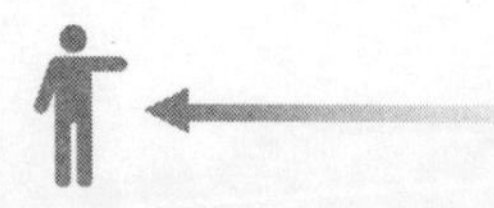

@daddydoubts,
@gfishandnuggets
@saltymamas
@SnarkyMommy78
@whatKatydidnext
@WTFpar3nt
@andy_park
@ryevenbark
@JeninLdnont
@hannyvanarkel
@EmmaSTennant
@braindad
@joeydonnas_gal
@wanderingWinter
@Debs_surfs
@AnecdtlBrthCtrl
@haisha99
@Stonecolddad316 and
pickled.plutonium.

About the Author

Nathan Joyce is the author of a number of popular books, including *A Celebration of David Attenborough: The Activity Book*, *The History of Insults*, *The Big Book of Trump* and *The Royal Geographical Society Puzzle Book*, and has contributed to many others, including *Chronologica: The Incredible Years that Defined History* and the hugely successful *Comedy Wildlife Photography Awards*. He lives in Brighton with his wife and son, and is just happy someone other than them likes his jokes.